★ Pictures Tell the Story

Storytelling Ideas for Teachers

By Jane Elling Haas

CPH ™
SAINT LOUIS

To Christian teachers everywhere

who tell the Good News of Jesus' saving grace

to students of all ages

Copyright © 1995 Concordia Publishing House
3558 S. Jefferson Avenue, St. Louis, MO 63118-3968
Manufactured in the United States of America

1 2 3 4 5 6 7 8 9 10   04 03 02 01 00 99 98 97 96 95

Contents

New Testament Bible Story Illustrations

Introduction

❏ What Is Storytelling?

For centuries people have told stories about family members and events and have passed down special teachings from one generation to another. Our Lord Jesus was the Master Storyteller. While He lived on earth, He gathered people wherever He went to tell them of the heavenly Father's love, illustrating principles and commandments with anecdotes and stories in order to teach people. We call these teaching stories *parables,* earthly stories that have a heavenly meaning.

Telling stories to one another is the most common and the most effective way of communicating ideas. Telling the chronological facts of an event in an interesting, appealing way is simple and easy for some, but complicated and difficult for others.

Our goal is to learn more about storytelling, the skills a good storyteller acquires and uses, different methods of telling the same story, and ways to enhance storytelling with visual aids. Stories in words and pictures have a lasting effect on the listeners.

As Christian leaders, we have an important impact on children and adults of all ages when we tell a story effectively. In our role, there are times for sharing with large groups, small groups, and with individuals. In each situation, we have an opportunity to share the Good News of God's saving love for us through Jesus. In each situation, we can tell stories.

By telling stories of Jesus' loving action for all people, we share God's love, communicate the Gospel as Jesus commanded (Matthew 28:19), and actively live our faith.

❏ Goals of a Storyteller

O my people, hear my teaching;
    listen to the words of my mouth.
I will open my mouth in parables,
    I will utter hidden things, things
        from of old–
what we have heard and known,
    what our fathers have told us.
We will not hide them from their children;
    we will tell the next generation
the praiseworthy deeds of the LORD,
    his power, and the wonders he has
        done.
He decreed statutes for Jacob
    and established the law in Israel,
which he commanded our forefathers
    to teach their children,
so the next generation would know them,
    even the children yet to be born,
    and they in turn would tell
        their children.
Then they would put their trust in God
    and would not forget his deeds
    but would keep his commands.

Psalm 78:1–7

As we tell the stories God has given us in His Word, we will

- identify with the story we want to tell. We'll tell of God our Creator's love and care, of Jesus' love and forgiveness through His saving action, of the Holy Spirit's work in our hearts to keep us in faith.

- confess and witness to our Christian faith as we visualize what we want to tell our listeners.

- share stories that are important to us. Storytelling is a shared experience through which we develop and build relationships with our listeners, while creating a common tradition.

- share Christian values. At a level far deeper than just words, storytelling helps us communicate values and truths to our listeners that, through the power of the Holy Spirit, help them grow in faith.

❏ Prepare to Storytell—Practice for Better Storytelling

Be yourself. These are the best words of advice for a storyteller. God has graciously given us a variety of gifts to use in order to further His kingdom. Reflect on the gifts God has given you. In prayer, ask God to show you the areas in which you have the strength to do His work. Jot them down on paper. Thank God for His gifts and for His help as you serve Him. Ask Him to help you communicate His Word clearly through storytelling.

Remember that the story you are about to tell must be real. When it becomes real in your mind and heart, then you can make it real to the audience.

- Before telling a story, pray that the Holy Spirit will help you speak clearly, relate your words appropriately to the listeners, and effectively communicate your message.

- Discern the central message of the Bible story. What is God's action in this story? How did God show His love or care for the people? What did God do then and what does He do today for you and me? Emphasize the Gospel truth from each Bible story rather than the facts. Storytell in order to plant seeds of faith and to help them grow. Storytell to help a student's relationship with Jesus Christ develop and strengthen.

- Become so familiar with the story that it becomes part of you. Read and review it ahead of time repeatedly. Practice by telling the story to a family member, a friend, or to yourself by using a mirror and an audio- or a videocassette recorder. Practice, practice, practice.

- Speak clearly. Read aloud directly from the Bible. Tell a Bible story naturally. Make sure you can pronounce names and present the events in the correct sequence. Tell the Bible story as God tells it in His Word without embellishing and creating extravagant details.

- Know the story so well that you can maintain eye contact with your students. Listeners will be good listeners if they see you looking at them rather than at a book or at a guide.

- Vary the pitch, tone, and volume of your voice. As you review a story, decide which parts need solemn, quiet, whisperlike expressions, and which parts require excited, loud, vocal expressions.

- Make the Bible story come alive by relating it to the lives of your students. For example, talk about how happy and thankful they are when a family member or a friend gets well. Relate those feelings to those of the official when Jesus healed his son. Applications help your students relate Jesus' teachings to their lives.

- Use visual words. Nouns and verbs usually work best. Too many adjectives can clutter the description. For example, it is interesting for the middle-grade listener to imagine the action in this story: King David's army marched into the field to fight Israel and Absalom's army. Twenty thousand men died in that day's battle. Absalom rode his mule and met his father's men. As Absalom's mule ran under thick branches of a large oak tree, Absalom's head got caught in the tree. He was left hanging, while his mule kept running (2 Samuel 18:6–9).

- Use auditory words. When you tell about God delivering the city of Jericho into Joshua's hands, use words such as march, blow the trumpets, and give a loud shout (Joshua 6). Have the children roleplay the words at the appropriate times in the story.

- Bridge the love, care, and salvation God showed His people long ago to the everyday lives of the students. For example, just as God took care of His

helper Paul as he traveled and told people about God's love and forgiveness, so God watches over you and keeps you in His loving care. He helps you, too, as you travel away from your homes. God keeps you safe, just as He kept Paul safe when the ship wrecked and the soldiers wanted to kill him. God still had work for Paul to do. God has work for you to do and helps you too (Acts 27–28).

- Let students be active participants. Have them finish a sentence. They might ring bells every time they hear you say "angels." Have young listeners echo short story sentences. Have them help set simple story sentences to a familiar melody and sing the story together as a class. Ask middle- and upper-grade students to help prepare, show, and save the picture helps suggested in this book. Some might create their own illustrations, booklets, audio- and videocassettes, or costumes and props to review and retell the Bible story for another class.

Your face, voice, eyes, and body movements demonstrate your interest and enthusiasm. Sometimes visuals and other helps are not needed. Show and tell the story in your words and actions.

❏ Age-Appropriate Storytelling Hints

A two-year-old might give you only two minutes of attention. That's typical. Tell very short Bible stories to very young children. Gauge the length of your story to the age of the audience. The hard part is condensing a Bible story into four minutes for four-year-olds or five minutes for five-year-olds. Just tell the highlights of a Bible story to very young children. As they grow older, details can be added. Remember to emphasize what you want remembered in simple words: God's love, care, and protection; forgiveness; the Gospel; the cross; Jesus' saving grace.

Very young children (ages 1 through 3) like to hear brief, simple Bible stories about Jesus in short sentences. They can begin to develop an attitude of joyful praise and thanks to Jesus for His friendship, for His coming as a little baby to be their Savior (though they don't understand *Savior* yet), and for His care for them and their families. They don't need explanations or backgrounds of biblical people and events. Do explain words such as *manger, friend,* and *family* as you use them.

Prekindergarten children (ages 4 and 5) like to hear brief Bible stories in short sentences. They enjoy hearing a big, important word and learning its meaning in the context of the story. For example, "Jesus' helpers in the boat were terrified! They were afraid of the stormy wind and lightning." Prekindergartners enjoy echoing short story sentences, supplying a missing word, singing simple Bible story words to familiar piggyback tunes, and illustrating Bible stories with their own pictures.

Kindergarten and primary level children (ages 6 through 8) like to hear Bible stories with a few challenging words they can help to define. They enjoy keeping word books. Have one student print the special word, and ask another to draw a pic-

ture to explain it. Stories should be no more than six or seven minutes long in order to keep their attention. They also like to review a Bible story by writing and illustrating their own versions and compiling the stories into booklets for the classroom. You can also have the students paint a story mural as a review activity.

Junior level students (ages 9 and 10) are usually able to listen to a longer Bible story, up to about 10–12 minutes. They will understand the roles of the characters and the sequence of events. Often they are able to retell the Bible story from the previous week. This group thoroughly enjoys roleplaying to review and retell Bible stories.

A storyteller will keep the interest and attention of **preteen level students (ages 11 and 12)** by being very well-prepared, correlating the Bible story truths with real events in the students' lives. Encourage the students to participate, and use visual helps. Ask your preteen students to help make storytelling visuals. They are creative and like to be in charge of special projects.

It's extra challenging to tell Bible stories to **junior high students (ages 13 and 14).** Many have heard or have read the Bible story before, and it isn't cool to want to hear it again. Tell the Bible story, or read it directly from the Bible. You might have the students follow along in their own Bibles as you read aloud. (Reading aloud to junior, preteen, and junior high students is an excellent way to model reading and language skills.) Spend the majority of your 10–15 storytelling minutes relating the Bible story and its truths to a situation or an event close to your students' experience. Let them practice the art of storytelling in small groups. Have them draw Bible stories from a basket, practice telling them, making their own visuals, and presenting their stories to younger children.

❏ Helps in This Book

Some stories include very simple line drawings of people and objects. Others include illustrations that involve movement, sequencing, and adding parts of the drawing as you storytell. Practice and adapt ideas to fit the needs of your students. Remember to involve them in preparing illustrations, completing illustrations during storytelling, and using illustrations to review Bible stories. They can be encouraged to make their own storybooks, puzzles, and games.

You might photocopy each Bible story page in order to set up a story file system. Place each photocopy in a separate file folder labeled with the Bible story title. This would be similar to a picture file in teaching.

God, our Father, has written the stories in the Bible for us to read, learn, and share. The key ingredients, the very best stories, are here for us already. We need not create them. We need not embellish them. We need only to *tell* them.

Through a storyteller's imagination, each Bible story comes to life and seems real to the listener as he/she hears God's Word, watches the illustrations give action to the story, and leaves with a better understanding of what God's Word means in his/her life today.

I pray that you will enjoy becoming a good storyteller/illustrator as you use your gifts to glorify God and plant seeds of His Word in the hearts of many listeners.

God Made Our Beautiful World

Genesis 1:1–2:3

Story Boards in Sequence

For young children, do not be concerned about the numerical day on which God created specific things, rather emphasize God's wonderful creation and His happiness with His world, of which we are a part.

Older students enjoy putting the days of creation in sequential order and like to make their own creation booklets to review and retell the Bible story.

Before class, obtain eight pieces of white poster board. As you tell the Bible story, use large, colorful markers or paint and a paintbrush for illustrating.

On the first poster, show night time by using black or dark blue paint. Show daytime by using bright yellow. Illustrate day and night by coloring big sections of the poster board in contrasting colors.

On the second poster, illustrate a beautiful sky using blue and pink colors; add fluffy white clouds.

On the third poster, draw majestic mountains, rolling hills, and valleys. Show water in an ocean, river, and stream. Add trees, bushes, plants, flowers, and fields of crops.

On the fourth poster, show the lights God placed in the sky—the stars, sun, and the moon.

On the fifth poster, illustrate living creatures—fish and amphibians in water and birds in the sky.

On the sixth poster, draw various animals living on the land (domestic and wild). Add a figure of a man and a woman at appropriate times in the story.

On the seventh poster, draw a large happy face to signify that God was happy with His creation. He blessed the seventh day and made it holy, a day of rest.

The Fall into Sin/ God Promises a Savior

Genesis 2:8–3:24

Story Picture Puzzle

Begin with a large piece of white poster board and colorful markers. Divide the poster in half for this storytelling illustration.

Draw simple trees and bushes for the Garden of Eden. In the middle of the garden draw one tree to represent the tree of life and another tree to represent the tree of the knowledge of good and evil. Draw Adam, the first man, in the garden. Print his name in uppercase and lowercase letters so that the children can identify him. Draw various animals around Adam, both in the air and on the ground. Draw a woman beside Adam. Print the word *woman* in uppercase and lowercase letters.

Continue by drawing a snake near Adam and Eve.

Draw a piece of fruit, such as a peach, an apple, or an orange, on the tree of the knowledge of good and evil.

Draw the same kind of fruit in Eve's hand and in Adam's hand.

As you tell about their shame, draw larger bushes to hide Adam and Eve.

Print the name *Eve* beside the woman and the name *Adam* beside the man. Draw sad faces on both Adam and Eve.

On the second half, draw Adam and Eve outside the garden. Show them wearing clothing.

Draw a large cross between Adam and Eve.

Draw a big red heart on the cross. Print *Jesus* on the heart as you tell how God promised a Savior for all people. The Savior, Jesus, came to die for everyone's sins and won the victory over sin, death, and the devil.

God kept His promise. He still loved Adam and Eve and cared for them. Draw smiles on their faces.

After illustrating the Bible story, cut the poster into sections (4 or 5 for young children, 6 to 10 for primary-age children). Have them put the puzzle picture together as they retell the story.

Story Rubbing of Jesus' Face

Enlarge the illustration of Jesus' face on a large piece of poster board. At least 24 hours before class time, run a line of white glue over the lines in the drawing of Jesus' face. Let the glue dry completely. (If stored carefully, this glue-line illustration can be used many times.) Cover the poster board illustration with a large piece of paper.

Tell how God continued to love His people. He kept His promise and sent Jesus to be our Savior. Jesus died and came alive again to give us life in heaven with Him. As you tell about Jesus, use the flat side of a crayon or a piece of dark colored chalk to rub gently and carefully over the glue lines on the paper. The children can watch the Savior's face appear.

God Saves Noah and His Family

Genesis 6:1–9:17

Chalk Talk

Use colored chalk to illustrate parts of this Bible story on the chalkboard.

Draw faces with frowns to represent unhappy, sinful people.

Draw a face to represent Noah. Below Noah's face draw a heart with a cross inside to show Noah's faithfulness to the Lord.

Draw the faces of Noah's wife, his three sons, and their wives as you tell how God kept them safe inside the ark.

Using the sides of the chalk, create a beautiful rainbow as you tell about God's promise to Noah. Use the following colors from the bottom to the top: red, orange, yellow, green, blue, indigo, and violet.

Draw a large red heart with a cross inside. Remind children that we can trust God to keep His promises to us too. Thank Him for His love and care and for sending Jesus to be our Savior.

God Makes a Promise to Abraham

Genesis 12:1–9; 15:1–6

Echo Pantomime Story

Have students repeat each story line. Show each illustration as the story unfolds.

Abraham and Sarah and nephew Lot
Loved our God and pleased Him a lot.
△

    Show an illustration of
    Abraham, Sarah, and Lot.

But most of the people where Abraham lived
Loved money and idols and prayed to them.
△

    Show many people's
    faces, coins, and statues.

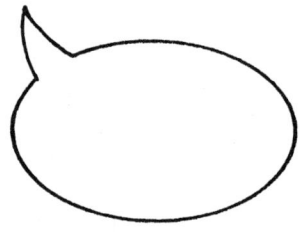

They prayed to the stars. They prayed to the moon.
They prayed to the sun from morning till noon.
△

    Show the stars, the moon,
    and the sun.

Then God came to Abraham and said to him,
"Take all that you own. Say good-bye to your friends.
I'll show you a land that's far, far away.
I'll bless your family with children some day."
△

    Show Abraham with a large
    speech bubble next to him
    to represent God's voice.
    Show hills and trees and
    a river. Show a number
    of children.

"And one of those sons in your family,
Many years from now the Savior will be."
△

    Show Jesus and print
    His name, Jesus, Savior

They traveled through deserts and over the hills.
God kept them safe from danger and ills.
They came to a land where the grass was green.
The trees had fruit, and the rivers were clean.
△

    Show fruit on the trees. Color the grass
    green and the water blue.

This beautiful land where God had led
Was a country called Canaan. "It's a gift," God said.
△

    Print Canaan near the grass and water.

"Your children will live on the land you see.
I'll bless you and make a great family."
Abraham built an altar there.
He thanked the Father for His love and care.
△

    Give Abraham a big smile.
    Show large trees and an altar of stones.

 Later God spoke to Abraham in a vision.
"Don't be afraid. I am your greatest treasure."
    Show Abraham and the speech bubble to represent God.
"God, I have no children yet.
Who will get all my land and my cattle?"
    Show a big question mark.
God told His friend to go outside
And look up into the deep dark sky.
"See the heavens. Count the stars.
I will bless you with that many in your family."
    Show Abraham with a big smile. Above him, show many stars.
God always keeps His promises.

God Takes Care of Joseph and His Brothers

Genesis 37–45

Create Joseph's Coat

Draw a figure of a young man, Joseph, on a piece of white poster board. As you tell about Joseph, the favorite son of his elderly father, Jacob (Israel), use bright paint colors to create his beautiful coat.

Crayon Resist Surprise Drawings

Before class, use a white crayon on white paper to illustrate Joseph's dreams, one per paper. As you storytell, paint over the drawings, one at a time, with dark watercolor or medium tempera paint. The illustration will appear where the crayon has resisted the paint.

Show Joseph's sheaf of grain standing upright. Show eleven sheaves of grain bowing to the upright sheaf.

Show Joseph. Show the sun, moon, and 11 stars near Joseph. Slant the stars, moon, and sun as if they are bowing to Joseph.

Story Illustrations

Draw a deep cistern (well). Draw Joseph's sad face at the bottom of the cistern.

Draw Jacob weeping when he hears of Joseph's death.

Draw a large Egyptian house. Show Joseph inside.

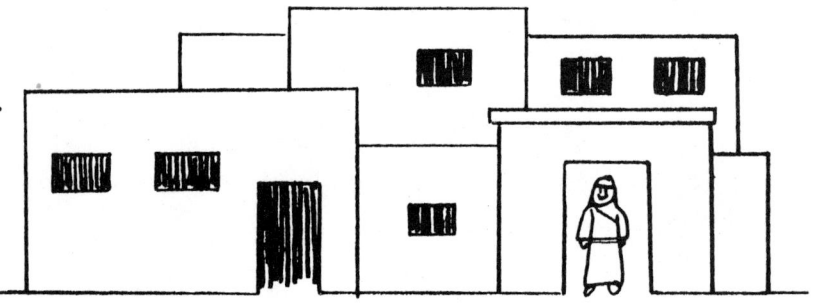

Crayon Resist Surprise Drawings

Using white crayon on white paper, illustrate the dreams of the cupbearer and the baker. On one paper, draw a vine with three branches. Show many clusters of grapes. Draw a cup filled with grape juice. Paint over this drawing with watercolor or tempera when you tell about the cupbearer's dream. On a second paper, draw a man with three baskets of bread on his head. Show birds eating the bread from the top basket. Paint over this drawing when you tell about Joseph interpreting the baker's dream.

Use the same crayon resist method to tell about the Pharaoh's dream of seven fat cows and seven thin cows, and of the seven full heads of grain and the seven scorched heads of grain.

Word Illustration

When you tell about Joseph meeting and forgiving his brothers, draw figures for Joseph and his 11 brothers. Print one letter of the sentence *I forgive you* above each of the people's heads. (Place the *I* above Joseph and continue left to right.)

(Joseph)   (his 11 brothers)

God Takes Care of Moses

Exodus 1–4

Accordion Paper Illustrations

Fold a large piece of white construction paper into four sections. Tape a second piece to the first if you want to add more scenes. As you storytell, draw each scene with colorful markers.

Draw baby Moses lying in a basket. Show the basket floating in the river. Add green plants and reeds. Then add the princess.

Draw toddler Moses with his mother and his sister Miriam.

Draw grown-up Moses with a few sheep. Draw a bush with flames near Moses. Draw his sandals. Draw Moses' hands covering his face. Add God's speech bubble with the words, "I will be with you."

Draw a figure of Moses holding a staff. As God speaks to Moses, add Moses' mouth, ears, and eyes. In a speech bubble above Moses, print, "But . . ." In God's speech bubble, print, "I will help you." Color the staff as you tell that God gave Moses the staff so he could perform miraculous signs.

God Helps His People Live Together

Exodus 15:22–16:36; 19:1–20:21

Chalk Talk

Tell the story as you draw the corresponding scene.

God saved His people when He made a dry path through the Red Sea.

Draw a cloud in the sky to represent God.

God led His people into the desert.

Draw many people following Moses. Draw a staff in Moses' hand.

The people became hungry. They couldn't find water. They complained to Moses.

Draw angry faces on the people.

Moses talked to God. God promised to stay with His people and take care of them.

Draw an arrow from Moses to God. Draw an arrow from God to Moses.

That evening, God sent birds so the people would have meat.

Draw birds in the sky.

The next morning, the people woke up and found the ground covered with white food. It was manna, a food that tasted like cake and honey.

Draw pieces of manna on the ground.

God made sure His people had water wherever they went.

One time, God told Moses to put a piece of wood in bad water. God made the water good to drink.

Draw a piece of wood in a small pool of water.

Another time, God made good water come out of a rock!

Draw a large rock and show water flowing from it.

God showed His people that He was with them. He met with them at Mount Sinai. He showed He was there with smoke, fire, and with the sound of a trumpet.

Draw a mountain. Show a cloud of smoke, flames of fire, and trumpet blasts coming from the mountain. Show a crowd of people next to the mountain.

Sometimes the people complained and fought with each other. God became angry. When His people did bad things, God punished them.

Draw a cloud to represent God, and give it a sad mouth to represent God's sadness and anger. Show people near the cloud, each with a sad face.

God loved His people all the time. When the people were sorry, He forgave them. He wrote the Ten Commandments on two special pieces of stone so His people would remember what He wanted them to do. God always loved and cared for His people.

Draw a cloud for God and show people near it. Draw a staff to represent Moses. In Moses' other hand, draw two stone tablets to represent the Ten Commandments.

God Makes Samson Strong

Judges 13–16

White on Black Chalk Talk

Draw the story illustrations with white chalk on pieces of black construction paper. You might draw all the illustrations before class, then add a detail to each as you tell the story.

Draw a statue, then draw a few people bowing to it.

Draw people praying to God.

Draw an angel with a man and a woman. Draw a baby in the woman's arms.

Draw a figure of Samson with his long hair.

Show Samson and Delilah.

Show Delilah talking to Samson's enemies. Show one enemy cutting the sleeping Samson's hair.

Draw Samson between two large pillars of a building.

Draw Samson pushing against the pillars and the pillars cracking and falling to pieces.

23

God Blesses Ruth

Ruth 1–4

Flip-a-Story Chart

As you tell this story, use a flip chart and colorful markers to illustrate the ways that God blessed Ruth.

Print *God's Blessings to Ruth* on the first page.

Stop occasionally during your storytelling to ask, "What blessing did God give to Ruth?"

Illustrate each blessing on a page and add a word that describes the illustration.

David Praises God

1 Samuel 17:33–37; Psalm 23

Chalk Talk

Use colored chalk to illustrate the story on the chalkboard as you tell it.

Draw a hillside with many sheep.

Add rocks, bushes, trees, and flowers. Draw the sun shining in the sky. Draw a brook or river in the foreground.

Add a stick figure for David.

As you tell about the work of a shepherd, draw an angry lion near the sheep to represent the threat of danger.

Draw David carrying a sheep to safety.

Draw David resting on the hillside.

Draw a lyre (stringed musical instrument) and musical notes when you tell how David sang praises to the Lord.

Jonathan and David

1 Samuel 17:55–20:42

Jesus Bandages

Make a large paper bandage from poster board. Make individual bandages from white paper, or use purchased bandages from the store, to illustrate that even though friends sometimes do things that hurt us, Jesus never hurts us. He loves us, protects us, heals our hurts, and forgives us when we say we're sorry that we hurt others.

Paper Doll Story Figures

Cut paper doll figures of David and Jonathan. Use a fine-tipped marker to create their features. Attach each figure to a craft stick and secure it in a lump of clay. Use a shoe box as the king's palace, create a street outside the palace using Legos or other blocks, and make a hiding place for David from an oatmeal container.

JONATHAN

DAVID

God Gives King Solomon a Wise Heart

1 Kings 3:1–15

Colored Chalk Talk

Use colored chalk on the chalkboard.

Draw stick figures of King David and Solomon, father and son.

Draw a crown on David's head. Then erase King David to show that he died.

Draw a crown on Solomon's head.

Draw a large tent church and add many stick figures to represent the people. Draw an altar and add drawings of the gifts (money, jars, jewelry).

Draw Solomon sleeping with a smile on his face.

Draw Solomon waking from his dream, with a smile on his face and a robe on his shoulders. Draw many happy faces around King Solomon.

God Sends Fire and Rain from Heaven

1 Kings 18:16–46

Colored Chalk Talk

Present a chalk talk while making colorful chalk drawings on the chalkboard or on newsprint.

Draw Elijah.

Draw King Ahab with a crown on his head.

Add a frown to King Ahab's face.

Draw a group of people to represent the people of Israel meeting Elijah on the mountain.

Draw the prophets of Baal bowing to an altar of stones.

Add a sun in the sky to show they prayed all day, morning, noon, and evening.

Draw 12 stones, and show Elijah kneeling at the altar he built.

Draw simple praying hands to represent Elijah praying to God.

Draw red and orange flames on Elijah's altar.

Draw clouds in the sky. Add drops of rain.

A Servant Girl Helps Her Master, Naaman

2 Kings 5

Story Illustrations

Use chalk on a chalk-board, markers on paper or poster board, or crayons on newsprint to illustrate the story scenes.

Draw Naaman. Give him a sword, shield, and helmet to show that he was the commander of an army.

Draw a few blotches on Naaman's arms and legs to represent leprosy.

Draw a young girl beside a woman.

Draw 10 silver coins and many, many gold coins. Draw 10 robes to represent the clothing. Beside these things, draw a letter with handwriting on it.

Draw an angry face to represent the king of Israel.

Draw a happy face to represent Elisha. Print the name *Elisha* beside it.

Print a large numeral 7.

Draw an angry face on Naaman.

Draw a few people beside Naaman to represent his servants.

Point to the numeral 7 when you tell about Naaman washing seven times in the Jordan River.

Draw Naaman again, this time without blotches. Show him standing with his servants. Point to the many, many coins Naaman had taken with him. Draw Elisha beside them. Give them all happy faces.

God Helps Esther Save Her People

Esther 1–10

Magnetic Photo Album Picture Story

Before class, create a photo album collection of this Bible story's events and scenes. Illustrate one scene per page. Insert each illustration, in sequence, under the magnetic film. Include the following illustrations.

Show King Xerxes and Queen Vashti. Print their names beneath their pictures.

Draw faces of many young women.

Draw Esther. Print her name on this page.

Draw Mordecai sitting at the king's gate.

Draw two angry officers of the king in the doorway, conspiring to kill the king.

Draw two stick figures hanging from the gallows.

Draw a smile on Mordecai's face.

Draw Haman on a very high seat of honor. Draw a frown on his face as you tell how Mordecai refused to pay Haman honor.

Draw the king giving Haman his signet ring.

Draw a scroll representing the decree that all the Jews should be killed.

Draw Mordecai with torn clothing, ashes on his skin, and a large sad mouth.

Draw a cup and a line through it. Draw a loaf of bread and a line through it. These symbols represent Esther's order to fast for three days.

Draw Esther, the king, and Haman at a banquet table.

Draw an arrow to Haman showing that he would be the man hanged on the gallows he had prepared for Mordecai.

Draw the king and queen together.

Draw Mordecai, second in rank to the king, with an elaborate robe and ring.

God's Helper, Isaiah

Isaiah 6

Story introduction—Today we'll hear about a time when God spoke to a man and said, "I have chosen you." Let's listen and find out what happened.

Crayon Illustrations

Use crayons to illustrate the story on newsprint.

Present Isaiah as a stick figure.

Represent God with a circle for a head and wavy lines for a robe.

Show the angels by drawing stick figures. Change Isaiah's facial expressions from happy to scared to happy again. Show him as God's helper talking to a group of people.

Send Me! Personalized Card

Talk about what it means to be God's messenger. As you do, fold a piece of construction paper in half to form a card. Then fold the front of the card gently in half and cut out a heart shape. Take an instant print photo of each child. Glue or tape the child's photo on the inside of the card so that the photo shows through the open heart. Print *Send Me!* under the photo. Students can creatively decorate the front and the inside of the card. Encourage them to give the card to someone they want to share Jesus' love with.

God Talks to Jeremiah

Jeremiah 1

Visualize a Name

Tell the story using the Bible as your guide. Before you begin, print *Jeremiah* on the chalkboard. Every time you mention his name in the story, point to the name *Jeremiah* and have the children say it with you. This will help focus their attention.

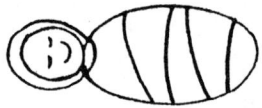

Draw a picture of a baby when you first tell about Jeremiah.

Draw a picture of a small boy when you tell about Jeremiah growing up.

Draw a picture of a man when you tell about Jeremiah talking to people as an adult.

Add other people listening to Jeremiah.

God Brings Jonah Back to Him

Jonah 1–4

Set the Scene

As you tell the story, cut large sections of blue and green sea from large pieces of construction paper. Make some waves larger than others. Cut a length of beige or brown paper to represent the shore. Stand these pieces along the chalk tray as you tell the story.

Chalk Talk

Use colored chalk to illustrate the story events.

Show Jonah running away from God.

Draw the large ship in which Jonah hid.

Show rain falling, waves splashing, Jonah falling off the ship, and Jonah inside the big fish.

Draw Jonah landing on the shore.

Show Jonah walking to Nineveh.

Show many people, with smiles on their faces, listening to Jonah.

God Saves Daniel's Three Friends

Daniel 3

Add a Part

Before class, use colorful markers to illustrate the following seven scenes on separate large pieces of paper. In each scene, leave something out that you will add during storytelling. As you tell the story, show each scene. Compile the scenes into a booklet for students to use to review the story later.

Show Shadrach, Meshach, and Abednego with colorful robes. Add their smiles and praying hands during storytelling.

Show the three friends with the king. During storytelling, add the king's crown, the three friends' smiles, and their praying hands.

Show people bowing and praying to a large statue with the three friends in the foreground. Add their smiles and praying hands.

Show the king and the three friends. Add the king's crown and his angry frown, as well as the friends' smiles and their praying hands.

Show the fiery hot furnace. Add stick figures lying down outside the furnace.

Show four men inside the furnace. Add the fiery orange and red flames inside the furnace, as well as the four friends' smiles and praying hands.

Show the king. Add his crown and a smile.

God Saves Daniel from the Lions

Daniel 6

Create a Story Mural

Before you tell the Bible story, make line drawings on the chalkboard with colorful chalk, or on a large piece of newsprint with colorful markers, to create a story mural. As you story-tell, involve students by having them draw the extra parts suggested for each illustration.

Draw Daniel. During the story, add his praying hands.

Draw the king. During the story, add a crown on his head and a gold belt around his robe.

Draw a group of the king's workers. During the story, draw frowns on their faces.

Draw a large rectangle to represent the entrance to a lions' den. During the story, draw faces of two or three lions.

Draw the king again. During the story, add a scroll in his hands to represent his new law.

Draw the lions. During the story, draw Daniel in the den with them. Cover the entrance to the lions' den by taping a large paper stone over the den.

On a separate paper, draw an angel in the lions' den beside Daniel. Don't show any lions' mouths in this picture. During the story, add the lions' closed mouths.

Draw a happy Daniel outside of the lions' den. During the story, add his happy smile.

Draw a few letters that the king wrote to people to tell them what God had done. During the story, write some of his words on the letters, such as *God saved Daniel* and *Daniel's God is the true God.*

John Is Born

Luke 1:5–25, 57–80

Simple Story Scenes

Draw the story with chalk on the chalkboard or with markers on large pieces of newsprint.

Draw a simple outline of the temple. Draw an altar inside the temple and add a figure to represent Zechariah. Add a figure for the angel.

Draw a second outline to represent the house where Zechariah and Elizabeth lived. Draw Elizabeth inside and add Zechariah, along with additional people as you tell the Bible story. Show Zechariah's mouth open and then closed tightly to show that he could not speak.

When you explain that baby John is born, draw a baby in Elizabeth's arms. Draw a slate in Zechariah's hands and print the name *John* on the slate. Draw smiles on all of their faces.

Jesus Is Born

Luke 2:1–7

Paint a Story

Tape a long length of paper to a wall. Mix several colors of tempera paint (or use premixed tempera) and have brushes and cleaning water handy.

Paint the story as you tell about Jesus' birthday.

Show Mary in a town called Nazareth.

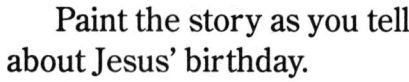

Paint an angel beside a smiling Mary.

Paint Mary and Joseph together in front of a house. Show them smiling.

Paint a soldier beside Mary and Joseph.

Paint Joseph leading a donkey with Mary on the donkey's back. Add a blanket and a knapsack.

Paint the outline
of Bethlehem and
the doorway of an inn.

Paint an innkeeper.
Paint Mary and Joseph
with sad faces.

Paint an outline of a
stable (a cavelike place)
with animals in it.

Paint Joseph near Mary.

Paint a baby in Mary's arms.

Paint a manger bed with straw.

Shepherds Worship Jesus

Luke 2:8–20

Draw and Sing a Story

Begin by drawing a simple manger and show baby Jesus lying inside it. Use marker and paper, or chalk and a chalkboard, to illustrate the story as you sing the words below to the tune of "Ten Little Indians." Draw simple stick figures for the shepherds and add smiling faces. Point to them as you sing the song a second and third time.

One little, two little, three little shepherds,
Four little, five little, six little shepherds,
Seven little, eight little, nine little shepherds,
* Run to find baby Jesus.

* For stanzas 2 and 3, substitute these endings: Come to worship Jesus; Go and tell of Jesus.

The Wise Men Visit Jesus

Matthew 2:1–12

Create a TV Story Roll

Hang a long section of paper horizontally on a wall or across a chalkboard. Use colorful markers or paint to illustrate as you storytell, drawing scenes from left to right. Be sure your paint is thick enough not to drip.

Show the stable with Mary, Joseph, and Jesus inside.

Draw a bright star in the sky above the stable.

Draw the Wise Men and camels, with gifts such as boxes and jars.

Draw the Wise Men (any number) traveling over deserts, rivers, and mountains.

Create a few scenes with the Wise Men traveling, both during the daytime and at night.

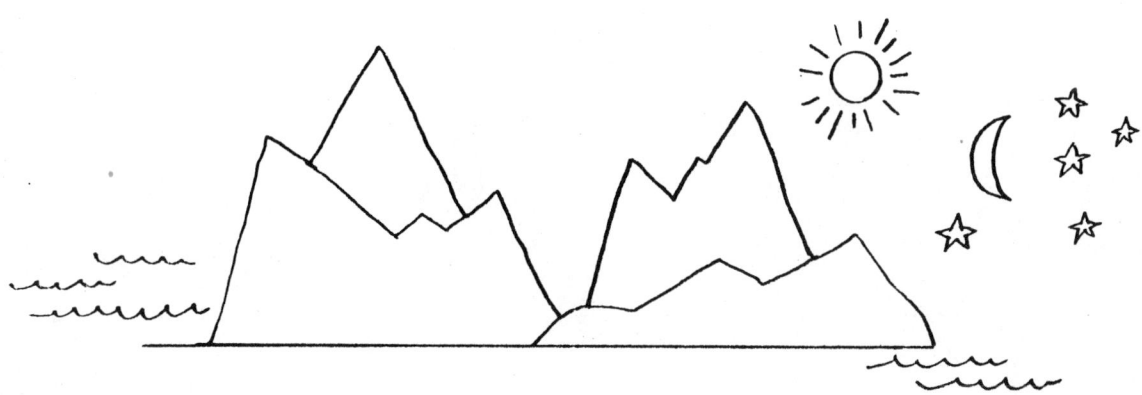

Show Mary, Joseph, and toddler Jesus in a house.

Draw the Wise Men visiting King Herod at his palace. Show Herod with an angry face.

Draw the Wise Men traveling again, with the bright star above them as their guide.

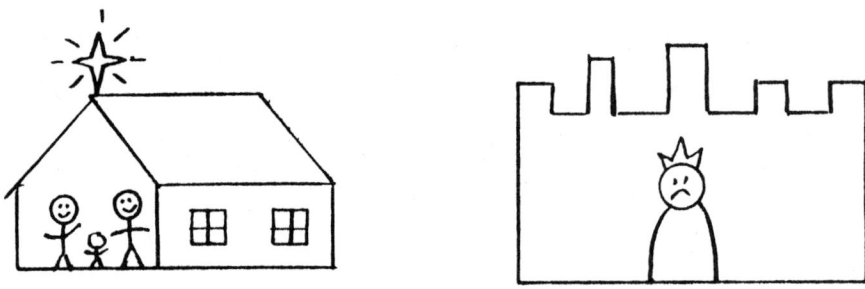

Show the bright star above the house where Jesus and His family lived. Show the Wise Men giving Jesus their gifts and worshiping Him.

Draw the Wise Men leaving, going home to their own lands.

If you painted, be sure to wait until your paint is thoroughly dry. Cut slits on opposite sides of a cardboard box. Cut out the front of the box to represent a TV. Insert the mural you created through the slot, from right to left, across the front of the TV opening. Adjust the mural so the beginning scene is inside the screen area. Gently pull the pictures toward the left as the children retell the Bible story.

Jesus and His Family Go to Egypt

Matthew 2:13–23

Continue the Mural

Tape a length of paper to the mural you created for the story about the Wise Men. Have colorful markers ready to use as you talk. Review the story of the Wise Men visiting and worshiping Jesus. Then continue the story by illustrating the following scenes.

Jesus, Mary, and Joseph sleeping in their house at Bethlehem at night.

An angel warning the Wise Men in a dream to go back to their homelands.

Soldiers standing by King Herod, who has an angry face because the Wise Men did not tell him where Jesus was located.

An angel warning Joseph in a dream to take his family to Egypt.

Joseph leading a donkey on which Mary and Jesus ride.

A dead King Herod.

An angel telling Joseph in a dream to go back to Israel.

Jesus, Joseph, and Mary with happy faces, standing by a house in their hometown, Nazareth.

John Baptizes Jesus

Matthew 3:13–17

Chalk Talk

Use paint on large newsprint, chalk on a chalkboard, or colorful markers on poster board to illustrate the story.

Crayon Resist Surprise Drawings

Draw the story pictures before class using white crayon on white paper. As you storytell, use a soft paintbrush to paint a blue wash of watercolor paint over each part of the story. The white illustrations will appear when the crayon resists the paint. Relate the importance of water and God's Word to our Baptism and our becoming God's children.

Jesus walked to the river.

Draw water for the river and a figure to represent Jesus.

God sent the Savior.

Color in a bright sky. Color in Jesus' hair, eyes, and clothing.

John the Baptizer met Jesus at the river.

Draw a figure to represent John.

They both walked into the water.

Draw John and Jesus in the river. To show them standing in water, color in the water, then add the upper half of their bodies above the water.

John baptized Jesus.

Draw three drops of water on Jesus' head.

God's Spirit came down from heaven in the form of a dove.

Draw a dove in the sky above Jesus.

As Jesus walked out of the water, God said, "This is My Son whom I love."

Show Jesus and John standing next to the water and smiling.

Jesus Calls the First Disciples

John 1:35–51; Matthew 4:18–22; Luke 6:12–19

Disciples Mural

Using colorful markers on newsprint, draw water to represent the Sea of Galilee.

Draw two men, the brothers Simon (Peter) and Andrew, holding a fishing net.

Draw Jesus near them with His arms outstretched.

Draw Jesus, Peter, and Andrew together.

Draw a fishing boat near the edge of the water.

Draw three more men, James, his brother John, and their father, Zebedee. They are all in the boat, holding fishing nets.

Show Jesus, Peter, and Andrew near the fishing boat. Show Jesus' arms outstretched.

Draw James and John next to Jesus and His helpers.

Draw Jesus praying near a mountainside. Add stars and a moon in the sky to represent the night.

Show the sun in the sky

to represent the day. Draw Jesus standing. One by one, draw 12 helpers beside Jesus: Simon Peter, Andrew, James, John, Philip, Bartholomew, Matthew, Thomas, James (son of Alphaeus), Simon the Zealot, Judas (son of James), and Judas Iscariot (the traitor).

Jesus Changes Water into Wine

John 2:1–11

Faces and Feelings

As you tell the story and elaborate on the celebration, use a marker to draw a happy face on a paper plate. Draw a sad face on another paper plate to represent how the happy people became sad when the bridegroom ran out of wine. Show the happy face again at the time in the story when Jesus changed the water into wine.

Draw a Story Strip

On a long length of paper, first draw simple figures of people with smiling faces. Draw two figures larger than the others to represent Jesus and the bridegroom.

Draw happy, celebrating people; show the bridegroom with a very sad face. Draw Jesus and His mother, Mary, larger than the others. Make Mary's face sad.

Draw six stone water jars in a row. With a light blue marker, fill each of the water jars to the brim with water.

Draw Jesus and the bridegroom. Draw a cup in the bridegroom's hand. With a red or purple marker, fill the cup with wine.

Draw many smiling faces as you finish telling about the miracle Jesus performed.

Draw bright yellow rays of sunshine around Jesus to represent His glory revealed.

Draw hearts in the disciples' chests to represent their faith in Jesus.

The Forgiving Father

Luke 15:11–32

Paper Plate Character Illustrations

Before class, draw pig faces on small pink paper plates.

Use colorful markers on three white paper plates to illustrate the characters of this Bible story.

Draw a sad face on one side of a paper plate as you tell about the younger brother asking his father for his inheritance.

Draw a sad face on one side of the second paper plate to represent the sad father who said good-bye to his son.

Tape the pig faces to the wall beside you as you hold the sad face of the younger brother and tell how he lived and ate with the pigs.

Draw a happy face on the opposite side of the father's paper plate and show it when you tell about the father running to welcome his son home.

Draw a happy face on the opposite side of the younger son's paper plate to show his happiness at his father's forgiveness.

Draw an angry face on the third paper plate to represent the older son's feelings about the celebration as a result of the younger son's return.

YOUNGER SON

FATHER

OLDER SON

Draw a happy face on the opposite side of the older son's paper plate at the end of the story, when the father explains that "you are always with me, and everything I have is yours. But we had to celebrate and be glad, because this brother of yours was . . . lost and is found."

Jesus Feeds 5,000 People

Matthew 14:14–21; Mark 6:30–44; John 6:1–15

Flip-a-Story Chart

Use markers on pages of a flip chart to illustrate the following scenes.

Show Jesus sitting in a boat in the middle of a lake and many people along the shore waiting for Jesus.

Show Jesus standing on shore with His disciples and many people surrounding them.

Draw a young boy, with a basket in his hand, standing next to Jesus.

Draw five small loaves of bread and two small fish in the basket. Show a smile on Jesus' face. Print *Thank You, heavenly Father* across the top of this page.

Draw a page full of smiling faces to represent the people Jesus fed that day.

Draw 12 baskets full of leftover bread.

"THANK YOU, HEAVENLY FATHER"

Jesus Walks on Water

Matthew 14:22–33

Flip-a-Story Chart—Homemade Story Chart

Use a flip chart and colorful markers. You can make a story chart by punching holes in the tops of large pieces of construction paper. Tie the pages loosely together with colored yarn.

Draw a boat on a lake quite a distance from the land with Jesus' disciples sitting in the boat. Add oars on each side.

Draw Jesus, with praying hands, kneeling on a mountainside.

Draw stars and the moon in the sky. Add big waves on the lake and swirls in the sky to show high winds.

Draw Jesus walking on the water toward the boat. Draw frightened expressions on the disciples' faces.

Draw Peter walking on the water. Show a big wave coming closer to Peter.

Draw Peter's arms reaching out to Jesus and Jesus' arms reaching out to Peter.

Draw Peter and Jesus in the boat with the other disciples on a calm lake. Draw the sun rising in the sky. Draw smiling faces on Jesus and on all of His helpers.

Jesus Talks with a Rich Young Man

Mark 10:17–31

File Card Flip-a-Story

Before class, create a file card flip-a-story. Illustrate the following scenes, one per 4″ × 6″ file card. Put the cards in the correct order from top to bottom. Print a title card for the beginning and a *Bible Words* card for the ending. Punch two holes in the top of each card. Tie the cards loosely together using craft yarn or leather laced through the holes at the top. You can also attach a metal ring to each of the corners instead of using yarn. Allow space so that the cards can be flipped as you tell the story.

Draw Jesus facing a man who is kneeling.

Draw two tablets of stone to represent the Ten Commandments.

Draw a house, many cattle and sheep, bags of gold and silver coins, fields of grain, and any other items the rich man may have possessed.

Draw the rich man's face and show a sad mouth. Add a thought bubble filled with coins representing the riches he could not give up.

Draw 12 faces to represent Jesus' disciples. Show their amazed expressions.

Draw a camel with a threaded sewing needle beside it.

Draw Peter's face with an amazed expression.

Draw Jesus' face with a smile.

Jesus and Nicodemus

John 3:1–17

Colorful Marker Illustrations

As you tell the story, illustrate the following scenes and concepts. Use one piece of colored construction paper for each. Draw the figures with colorful markers.

Draw the faces of Jesus and Nicodemus. Print their names below their faces.

Draw an infant to represent Nicodemus' question in verse 4.

Draw a large question mark to signify Nicodemus' question in verse 9.

Draw a manger. Add baby Jesus. Draw a large cross and an empty tomb for verse 16.

For students in middle grades and older, draw a candle with a bright flame to represent Jesus, the Light of our world.

Jesus Heals an Official's Son

John 4:43–54

Crayon Rubbing—Surprise Pictures

Before class, illustrate each scene on a separate piece of white paper. Make a line of white craft glue over the lines in the illustrations. Allow the glue to dry completely overnight. Then place the illustrations in the correct order, with a clean piece of paper stapled or clipped to the top of each. As you storytell, gently rub the width of a peeled crayon over each illustration so that the glue lines appear. Tape each illustration to the wall to help students see the sequence of events.

Illustrate Jesus being welcomed by a number of people who represent the Galileans.

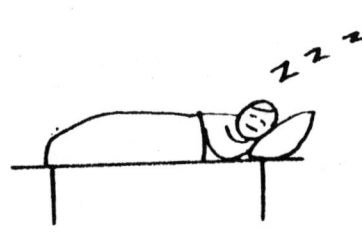 

Draw a sick boy lying on his bed.

Draw the official facing a few of his servants.

Draw the official facing Jesus.

Draw the official's happy face.

Print the words *Your son will live.*

"Your son will live."

The Parable of the Sower

Matthew 13:1–23; Luke 8:1–15

A Story Scroll to Unroll

Before class, illustrate this parable with colorful markers on a long scroll of paper. Plan to add some of the details as you storytell. Tape the left side of the scroll to a wall or tack it to a bulletin board. Gently unroll the scroll to the right. You might want to ask a helper to do the unrolling if you plan to add to the illustrations.

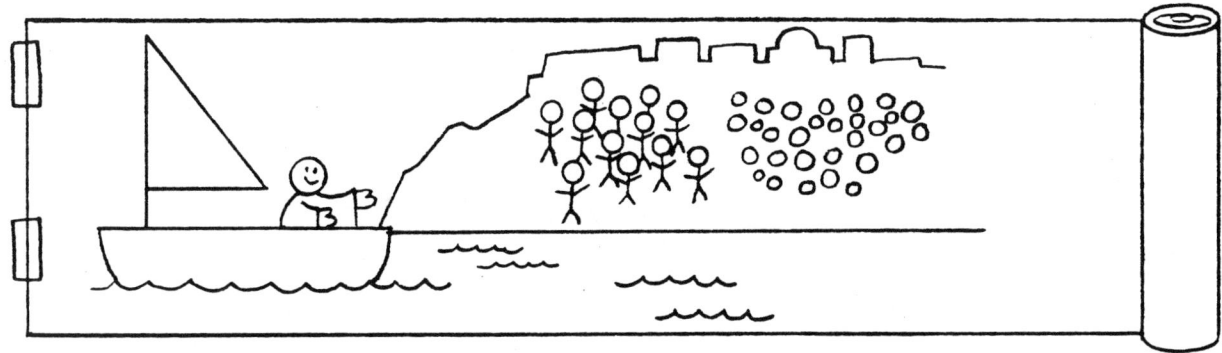

Show Jesus sitting in a boat on the lake. Show His 12 helpers standing on the shore. Show an outline of a town behind them. Add many people to represent the crowd of people who came to hear Jesus.

Illustrate a farmer with his arms extended, sowing seeds in a field. Show a path with footprints along it. Add birds on the path, eating the seeds.

Illustrate rocks of all sizes. Add seeds amid the rocks. As you storytell, draw a few small withered plants.

Illustrate a patch of brown and gray thorns. Show seeds on the thorns. Add green plants amid the thorns. Then draw more brown and gray thorns around and on top of the green plants, choking them of food and water.

Illustrate a field of rich, dark brown soil. Add seeds on the soil. Then draw little green plants all over the field. As you talk, show the green plants growing taller and sturdier.

Illustrate an open Bible and a few little seeds. Show your classroom Bible as you talk about the meaning of this parable (Luke 8:11–15).

Draw large red hearts beside the Bible. As you finish the parable's meaning, draw a happy face inside each heart to represent those who hear the Word, keep it in their hearts, and share it.

The Transfiguration of Jesus

Luke 9:28–36

Surprise Picture Message

Prepare a surprise picture. Before class draw a figure of Jesus on white paper. Use a cotton swab dipped in lemon juice to draw Moses and Elijah facing the figure of Jesus.

On a second piece of white paper, use the cotton swab dipped in lemon juice to print a simple message such as *This is My Son*.

As you tell about Jesus praying on the mountain with Peter, James, and John, use a paintbrush and yellow tempera to highlight Jesus' face and body.

Place a piece of cotton fabric (a handkerchief or remnant) on top of the surprise picture. Run a hot iron over it for five to ten seconds (do not use steam) so that the figures of Moses and Elijah appear beside Jesus.

Use a paintbrush and yellow tempera to highlight Moses and Elijah.

Finally, apply the hot iron over the cotton fabric and the second paper so that God's words appear. Fold back the drawings of Elijah and Moses so that only Jesus shows on the first paper.

The Parable of the Rich Fool

Luke 12:13–21

Light and Dark Chalk Talk

Use white chalk to illustrate the story on a large piece of black or dark blue construction paper.

Draw Jesus and a number of faces—or figures of people— around Him.

Draw a figure of the rich man. Add a thought bubble with a big question mark inside it.

Draw a few small barns. Cross these out with your chalk. Draw bigger barns. Draw baskets of corn, fruit, and vegetables beside the bigger barns.

Draw a smiling face for the rich man as he thinks about all his possessions.

Draw the rich man lying down, dead.

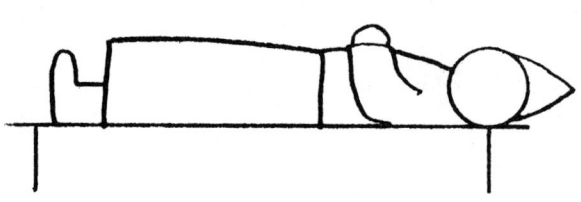

Jesus Prays in the Garden

Matthew 26:30–56; John 18:1–11

Chalk Talk

Use colored chalk to draw on the chalkboard.

Show nighttime by drawing a few stars and the moon in the sky.

Draw trees and a stone walk to represent the Garden of Gethsemane. Show a gate.

Draw Jesus and His 12 disciples outside the garden.

Show Jesus and 3 disciples inside the garden.

Draw Jesus further into the garden. Give Him a sad face. Draw His praying hands. Show Peter, James, and John with their eyes closed, sleeping.

When you tell about Jesus going to pray by Himself the third time, draw an angel next to Him.

Then draw Jesus with His 3 disciples, standing and awake.

Draw many angry faces in a group coming to take Jesus away.

Continue telling briefly what happened to Jesus, emphasizing that Jesus died and rose again, keeping His promise to save us from our sin.

Draw a cross.

Draw Jesus, alive and happy.

59

Jesus Died for All People/
Jesus Is Alive

Matthew 27:11–66; Luke 24:1–49

Easter Cross

Before class, cut out a large, brown paper cross. At the end of the story, when you tell of Jesus' becoming alive again, draw and color beautiful flowers. Glue them to the cross.

Story Scenes

Draw simple line drawings on the chalkboard. Gradually create a scene as you tell each part of the story.

Draw Jesus carrying the cross to Calvary.

Draw three crosses upright on the hill.

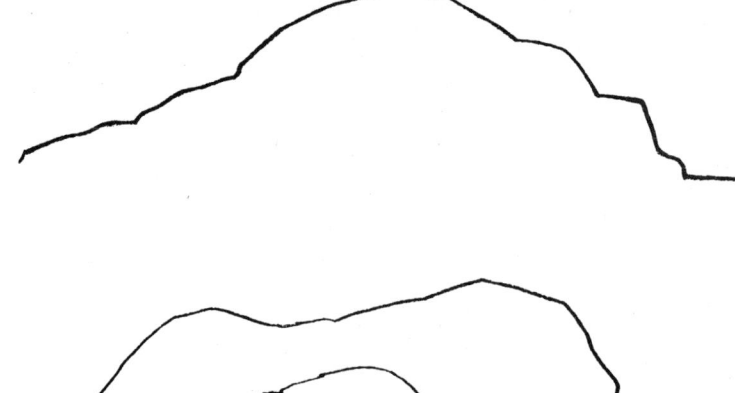

Draw a cave tomb with a large stone blocking the entrance; add sad people standing outside the tomb.

Draw happy people hearing that Jesus is alive again.

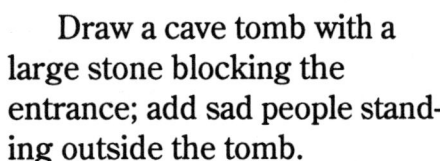

60

Chalk Rubbing—Surprise Picture

Draw simple line drawings, similar to the chalk drawings, on a sheet of poster board. Run a line of white glue over the penciled lines and let it dry thoroughly. Clip or tape a piece of paper over the entire glue drawing. As you tell the Bible story in class, gently rub the flat edge of a piece of colored chalk over the appropriate parts of your drawing. The picture will appear.

Abstract Concept Illustration for Older Students

Draw a simple line drawing of a flower bulb. You might use an amaryllis bulb or a tulip bulb as your example. As you say the following, use colorful markers or chalk to illustrate your example.

Does anyone know what this is? It's a flower bulb. If we plant this dried, dead-looking bulb in the ground, soon we'll get a wonderful surprise. We'll see little green sprouts growing. These sprouts will grow and grow until, after a while, a beautiful flower blooms.

This bulb and flower reminds us of Jesus. He died on the cross. Then His friends put Him into a grave. But on Easter Jesus' friends had a wonderful surprise. Jesus was alive!

Jesus Ascends into Heaven

Luke 24:50–53; Acts 1:1–11

Story in Motion

Use construction paper, markers, and scissors.

At the bottom of a strip of poster board, draw a figure of Jesus. Show a smile on His face. Draw His arms lifted in a gesture of blessing.

On a large piece of poster board, draw Jesus' 11 disciples. Show them standing on a hillside outside the small town of Bethany. Show smiles on their faces.

Cut a large white cloud from a piece of white construction paper. Glue or tape the cloud to the top of the hillside scene so that the cloud is half off the paper.

Cut a horizontal slit near the disciples. Cut a second horizontal slit near the bottom of the cloud. Insert the bottom of the poster board strip showing Jesus into the bottom slit. Insert the top of the strip into the slit in the cloud.

As you tell about Jesus rising into heaven, gently pull the strip upward to show Jesus disappearing behind the cloud.

Use a fine-tipped marker to change the disciples' smiles into expressions of wonder and amazement (draw circles for their open mouths).

The First Pentecost

Acts 1:1–14; 2:1–42

Chalk Talk

Before class, draw a simple outline of a house on the chalkboard. Using browns and grays, draw people inside the house.

At the appropriate time in the story, use red, orange, and yellow to add flames above the people's heads.

Alkaline Surprise Picture

At least a day before class, prepare a basket-style coffee filter to serve as the medium for your surprise picture. You might want to prepare one for each student (depending on their ages) to use as a review activity after the story.

Combine ¼ teaspoon tumeric powder (a spice) with ⅓ cup rubbing alcohol in a mixing bowl. Dip the whole coffee filter into the bowl. It will turn the color of goldenrod. Place the filter on newspaper to dry overnight.

Make ink by mixing one tablespoon water with one teaspoon baking soda in a plastic cup.

Use a cotton swab to draw a large flame with smaller flames around it on the flat side of the coffee filter. They will immediately turn red. (A chemical change occurs when the alkaline substance comes in contact with the chemicals in the filter paper).

If you have prepared a coffee filter for each student, let them create their own flames as you review the work of the Holy Spirit at Pentecost and in a Christian's life.